# NEVER GIVE UP

summersdale

NEVER GIVE UP

Copyright © Summersdale Publishers Ltd, 2017

All rights reserved.

No part of this book may be reproduced by any means, nor transmitted, nor translated into a machine language, without the written permission of the publishers.

Condition of Sale
This book is sold subject to the condition that it shall not, by way of trade or otherwise, be lent, resold, hired out or otherwise circulated in any form of binding or cover other than that in which it is published and without a similar condition including this condition being imposed on the subsequent purchaser.

Summersdale Publishers Ltd
46 West Street
Chichester
West Sussex
PO19 1RP
UK

www.summersdale.com

Printed and bound in the Czech Republic

ISBN: 978-1-78685-041-6

Substantial discounts on bulk quantities of Summersdale books are available to corporations, professional associations and other organisations. For details contact general enquiries: telephone: +44 (0) 1243 771107, fax: +44 (0) 1243 786300 or email: enquiries@summersdale.com.

To..............................

From..........................

**Never give up, for that is just the place and time that the tide will turn.**

Harriet Beecher Stowe

THERE IS NO FAILURE EXCEPT IN NO LONGER TRYING.

ELBERT HUBBARD

**You're alive!**
**You can achieve.**

CHARACTER
CONSISTS OF WHAT
YOU DO ON THE
THIRD AND
FOURTH TRIES.

James A. Michener

**SMOOTH SEAS**

**DO NOT MAKE**

**SKILFUL SAILORS.**

AFRICAN PROVERB

You can, you should,
and if you're brave
enough to start,
you will.

Stephen King

**YOU HAVE EVERYTHING YOU NEED.**

THINKING WILL NOT
OVERCOME FEAR,
BUT ACTION WILL.

W. Clement Stone

A MAN CAN SUCCEED AT ALMOST ANYTHING FOR WHICH HE HAS UNLIMITED ENTHUSIASM.

Charles M. Schwab

# IF YOU'RE GOING THROUGH HELL, KEEP GOING.

WINSTON CHURCHILL

WHEN SOMETHING
REALLY MATTERS,
YOU SHOULD NEVER
GIVE UP OR GIVE IN.

Gordon Brown

**Never consider the possibility of failure; as long as you persist, you will be successful.**

Brian Tracy

# IF AT FIRST YOU DON'T SUCCEED, TRY AGAIN.

There are no limits. There are only plateaus, and you must not stay there, you must go beyond them.

Bruce Lee

If you're walking down
the right path and
you're willing to keep
walking, eventually
you'll make progress.

Barack Obama

**Victory is sweetest when you've known defeat.**

Malcolm Forbes

ENERGY AND PERSISTENCE CONQUER ALL THINGS.

BENJAMIN FRANKLIN

DON'T LOAF AND
INVITE INSPIRATION;
LIGHT OUT AFTER IT
WITH A CLUB.

Jack London

FOLLOW YOUR
DREAMS. THEY
KNOW THE WAY.

KOBI YAMADA

# THE STRONGEST STEEL IS FORGED IN THE HOTTEST FIRE.

Proverb

# STICK WITH WHAT YOU LOVE.

Don't allow your mind to tell your heart what to do. The mind gives up easily.

Paulo Coelho

# EVERYTHING HAPPENS FOR A REASON.

THE BEST WAY

TO PREDICT

YOUR FUTURE IS

TO CREATE IT.

ABRAHAM LINCOLN

**One may walk
over the highest
mountain one
step at a time.**

John Wanamaker

IN ORDER TO
SUCCEED, WE MUST
FIRST BELIEVE THAT
WE CAN.

Nikos Kazantzakis

THROW CAUTION

TO THE WIND AND

JUST DO IT.

CARRIE UNDERWOOD

# FIGHT FOR WHAT YOU LOVE.

THE SEASON OF
FAILURE IS THE BEST
TIME FOR SOWING
SEEDS OF SUCCESS.

Paramahansa Yogananda

# Difficulties strengthen the mind, as labour does the body.

Seneca the Younger

FALL DOWN SEVEN
TIMES, STAND
UP EIGHT.

Japanese proverb

# EVERY GREAT ACHIEVEMENT WAS ONCE CONSIDERED IMPOSSIBLE.

**When it is darkest,
men see the stars.**

Ralph Waldo Emerson

**A TREE DOESN'T FALL WITH ONE BLOW.**

YIDDISH PROVERB

# DREAM BIG AND DARE TO FAIL.

Norman Vaughan

**If you never try,
you'll never know.**

**FREEDOM LIES**

**IN BEING BOLD.**

ROBERT FROST

**When everything seems to be going against you, remember that the airplane takes off against the wind, not with it.**

Henry Ford

YOU CAN'T GO
BACK AND MAKE
A NEW START, BUT
YOU CAN START
RIGHT NOW AND
MAKE A BRAND
NEW ENDING.

James R. Sherman

# WORK HARD, HAVE HIGH STANDARDS.

**TOUGH TIMES NEVER LAST, BUT TOUGH PEOPLE DO.**

ROBERT H. SCHULLER

**Courage isn't having the strength to go on – it is going on when you don't have strength.**

Napoleon Bonaparte

**Failure is the fuel to keep on achieving.**

VITALITY SHOWS
IN NOT ONLY THE
ABILITY TO PERSIST
BUT THE ABILITY TO
START OVER.

F. Scott Fitzgerald

**Still round the corner
there may wait,
A new road or
a secret gate.**

J. R. R. Tolkien

YOU DON'T
LEARN TO WALK
BY FOLLOWING
RULES. YOU LEARN
BY DOING, AND BY
FALLING OVER.

Richard Branson

GIVE YOURSELF

CREDIT WHERE

IT IS DUE.

I KNOW FROM
EXPERIENCE THAT
YOU SHOULD
NEVER GIVE UP
ON YOURSELF OR
OTHERS, NO
MATTER WHAT.

George Foreman

**BE BOLD, BE BOLD, AND EVERYWHERE BE BOLD.**

HERBERT SPENCER

**Things worth doing
are not easy.**

Our greatest glory
is not in never falling,
but in rising up every
time we fall.

Oliver Goldsmith

# KEEP
# GOING.

A JOURNEY OF A
THOUSAND MILES
BEGINS WITH A
SINGLE STEP.

Lao Tzu

**It's not that I'm so smart; it's just that I stay with problems longer.**

Albert Einstein

# DIFFICULT DOESN'T MEAN IMPOSSIBLE.

# NEVER GIVE UP, HAVE THE PASSION. DON'T BE AFRAID.

Barbara Broccoli

IT DOES NOT MATTER
HOW SLOWLY YOU
GO SO LONG AS
YOU DO NOT STOP.

Confucius

# TAKE EVERYTHING ONE STEP AT A TIME.

**THE MORE WE DO, THE MORE WE CAN DO.**

WILLIAM HAZLITT

**Even if you're on the right track, you'll get run over if you just sit there.**

Will Rogers

YOUR VICTORY IS
RIGHT AROUND THE
CORNER. NEVER
GIVE UP.

Nicki Minaj

# EVERY ARTIST
# WAS FIRST AN
# AMATEUR.

RALPH WALDO EMERSON

# YOU CAN'T BUILD A REPUTATION ON WHAT YOU ARE GOING TO DO.

Henry Ford

FAILURE
IS JUST A
STEPPING
STONE.

**People may doubt
what you say, but
they will believe
what you do.**

Lewis Cass

# TURN A SETBACK INTO A COMEBACK.

A CHAMPION IS
SOMEONE WHO
GETS UP WHEN
HE CAN'T.

JACK DEMPSEY

SUCCESS SEEMS
TO BE LARGELY
A MATTER OF
HANGING ON
AFTER OTHERS
HAVE LET GO.

William Feather

**DO ONE THING**

**EVERY DAY THAT**

**SCARES YOU.**

ELEANOR ROOSEVELT

Positive anything
is better than
negative nothing.

Elbert Hubbard

**Things can only
ever get better.**

**Never, never, never give up.**

Winston Churchill

**LEAP AND THE NET WILL APPEAR.**

JOHN BURROUGHS

# FAILURE IS A PART OF EVERY JOURNEY.

**SELF-TRUST IS THE FIRST SECRET OF SUCCESS.**

RALPH WALDO EMERSON

# YOUR ASPIRATIONS
# ARE YOUR
# POSSIBILITIES.

Samuel Johnson

NEVER GIVE UP... NO ONE EVER KNOWS WHAT'S GOING TO HAPPEN NEXT.

L. Frank Baum

**Life shrinks
or expands
according to
one's courage.**

Anaïs Nin

JUST DON'T QUIT.

THE MOST
EFFECTIVE
WAY TO DO IT
IS TO DO IT.

AMELIA EARHART

QUITTERS NEVER WIN,
WINNERS NEVER QUIT.

**WHENEVER YOU FALL, PICK SOMETHING UP.**

OSWALD AVERY

# NO ONE KNOWS WHAT HE CAN DO UNTIL HE TRIES.

Publilius Syrus

**Problems are not stop signs, they are guidelines.**

Robert H. Schuller

ONCE WE ACCEPT

OUR LIMITS, WE

GO BEYOND THEM.

ALBERT EINSTEIN

**It's never too late to be what you might have been.**

Adelaide Anne Procter

# INSTANT SUCCESS DOESN'T EXIST, BUT WORKING HARD DOES.

BE BRAVE
ENOUGH TO BE
YOUR TRUE SELF.

Queen Latifah

SHOOT FOR THE
MOON. EVEN IF YOU
MISS YOU'LL LAND
AMONG THE STARS.

Les Brown

# FORTUNE
# FAVOURS
# THE BOLD.

LATIN PROVERB

**Your past does not determine your future.**

LIFE ISN'T ABOUT
WAITING FOR
THE STORM TO
PASS... IT'S ABOUT
LEARNING TO
DANCE IN THE RAIN.

Anonymous

Opportunity dances
with those already on
the dance floor.

H. Jackson Brown Jr

# LIFE IS SIMPLE, IT'S JUST NOT EASY.

A successful man is one who can lay a firm foundation with the bricks others have thrown at him.

David Brinkley

EVER TRIED.
EVER FAILED.
NO MATTER.
TRY AGAIN.
FAIL AGAIN.
FAIL BETTER.

Samuel Beckett

**AN OBSTACLE**

**IS OFTEN A**

**STEPPING STONE.**

WILLIAM PRESCOTT

WE MUST
ACCEPT FINITE
DISAPPOINTMENT,
BUT WE MUST NEVER
LOSE INFINITE HOPE.

Martin Luther King Jr

**The greater the difficulty, the more glory in surmounting it. Skilful pilots gain their reputation from storms and tempests.**

Epicurus

# HALF THE FUN OF SUCCESS IS THE PURSUIT.

DON'T DIG UP IN
DOUBT WHAT YOU
PLANTED IN FAITH.

Elisabeth Elliot

**RULE YOUR MIND OR IT WILL RULE YOU.**

HORACE

The brave man is
not he who does not
feel afraid, but he who
conquers that fear.

Nelson Mandela

LOOK HOW
FAR YOU'VE
COME.

IT'S NOT WHETHER
YOU GET KNOCKED
DOWN, IT'S WHETHER
YOU GET UP.

Vince Lombardi

KEEP
TRYING.

**There is always a solution.**

I HAVE NOT FAILED.
I'VE JUST FOUND
10,000 WAYS THAT
WON'T WORK.

Thomas Edison

**BOLDNESS BE MY FRIEND!**

WILLIAM SHAKESPEARE

# EVERY ACCOMPLISHMENT STARTS WITH THE DECISION TO TRY.

**The question isn't who is going to let me; it's who is going to stop me.**

Ayn Rand

# ALL MY SUCCESSES
# HAVE BEEN BUILT
# ON MY FAILURES.

Benjamin Disraeli

# To dare is to lose one's footing momentarily. Not to dare is to lose oneself.

Søren Kierkegaard

IF YOU DON'T RUN YOUR OWN LIFE, SOMEBODY ELSE WILL.

JOHN ATKINSON

# GIVING UP IS NOT AN OPTION.

ONLY THOSE WHO
DARE TO FAIL
GREATLY CAN EVER
ACHIEVE GREATLY.

Robert F. Kennedy

THOSE WHO WISH

TO SING ALWAYS

FIND A SONG.

SWEDISH PROVERB

# YOU ARE NOT STUCK WHERE YOU ARE UNLESS YOU DECIDE TO BE.

Wayne W. Dyer

DON'T BE
DISCOURAGED;
THE LAST KEY
IN THE BUNCH
OFTEN OPENS
THE LOCK.

# YOU JUST CAN'T BEAT THE PERSON WHO WON'T GIVE UP.

Babe Ruth

**YOUR PAST IS NOT**

**YOUR POTENTIAL.**

BARBARA WINTER

**YOU ARE THE CREATOR OF YOUR FUTURE.**

WHERE THERE
IS A WILL, THERE
IS A WAY.

Proverb

**Only those who will risk going too far can possibly find out how far one can go.**

T. S. Eliot

YOU OWE IT
TO YOURSELF
TO CARRY ON.

# IF THINGS GO WRONG, DON'T GO WITH THEM.

ROGER BABSON

**THERE IS ALWAYS ROOM AT THE TOP.**

DANIEL WEBSTER

**You were put on this planet for a reason.**

**Doubt whom you will, but never yourself.**

Christian Nestell Bovee

ACT AS IF WHAT
YOU DO MAKES
A DIFFERENCE.
IT DOES.

William James

IN THE MIDDLE OF DIFFICULTY LIES OPPORTUNITY.

ALBERT EINSTEIN

**Setting goals is
the first step in
turning the invisible
into the visible.**

Tony Robbins

# YOU ARE CAPABLE.

TO CONQUER FEAR
IS THE BEGINNING
OF WISDOM.

Bertrand Russell

OPPORTUNITIES

MULTIPLY AS THEY

ARE SEIZED.

SUN TZU

# YOU HAVE A
# PURPOSE.

IF YOUR SHIP

DOESN'T COME IN,

SWIM OUT TO IT.

JONATHAN WINTERS

**Let your hook always be cast; in the pool where you least expect it, there will be a fish.**

Ovid

ERRORS... ARE
THE PORTALS
OF DISCOVERY.

James Joyce

# The gem
# cannot be polished
# without friction,
# nor a man perfected
# without trials.

Chinese proverb

**THE ROUGHEST ROAD OFTEN LEADS TO THE TOP.**

CHRISTINA AGUILERA

**If someone else can do it, so can you!**

# NO GREAT THING

## IS CREATED

## SUDDENLY.

EPICTETUS

# DON'T GIVE UP THE THINGS THAT MAKE YOU HAPPY.

I can't change
the direction of
the wind, but I can
adjust my sails to
always reach
my destination.

Jimmy Dean

NO ATTAINMENT
IS BEYOND HIS
REACH WHO
EQUIPS HIMSELF
WITH PATIENCE TO
ACHIEVE IT.

Jean de La Bruyère

OPTIMISM IS THE
FOUNDATION
OF COURAGE.

NICHOLAS M. BUTLER

# DIFFICULTY IS PART OF ACHIEVING SUCCESS.

**Man cannot aspire if he look down; if he rise, he must look up.**

Samuel Smiles

WHEN YOU COME
TO THE END OF YOUR
ROPE, TIE A KNOT
AND HANG ON.

Anonymous

**Hope is important because it can make the present moment less difficult to bear.**

Thích Nhất Hạnh

CHANGE YOUR
LIFE TODAY. DON'T
GAMBLE ON THE
FUTURE, ACT NOW,
WITHOUT DELAY.

Simone de Beauvoir

**If you don't,
someone else will.**

# LET PERSEVERANCE BE YOUR ENGINE AND HOPE YOUR FUEL.

H. Jackson Brown Jr

# HE CONQUERS

# WHO ENDURES.

PERSIUS

NEVER GIVE UP.

If you're interested in finding out more about our books, find us on Facebook at **Summersdale Publishers** and follow us on Twitter at **@Summersdale**.

**www.summersdale.com**

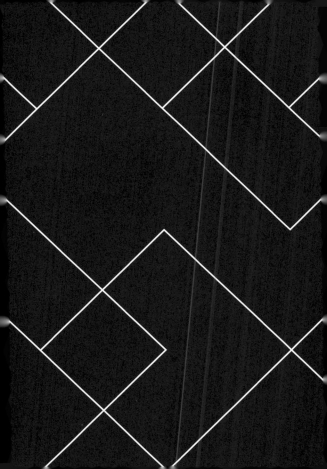

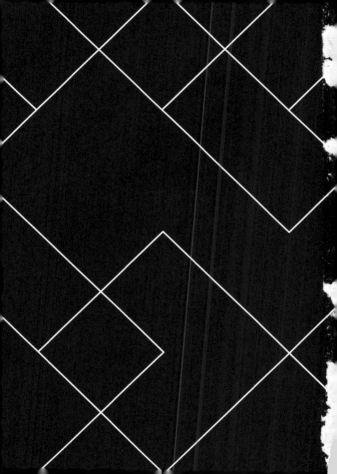

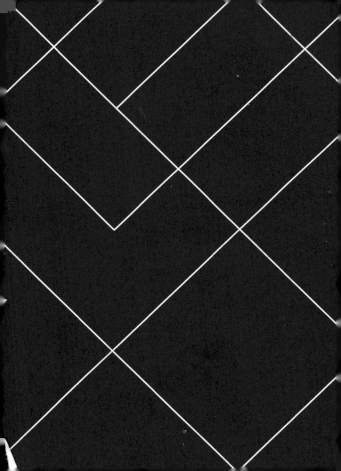